Fighter Planes

by Jay Schleifer

Capstone Press

MINNEAPOLIS

Printed in the United States of America.

Capstone Press • 2440 Fernbrook Lane • Minneapolis, MN 55447

Editorial Director   John Coughlan
Managing Editor   Tom Streissguth
Production Editor   James Stapleton
Book Design   Tim Halldin

Library of Congress Cataloging-in-Publication Data

Schleifer, Jay.
    Fighter planes / Jay Schleifer.
        p. cm. -- (Wings)
    Summary: Traces the history of fighter aircraft, focusing on the most significant models of the major world powers, and describes the "dream planes" of the future.
    Includes bibliographical references (p. 45) and index.
    ISBN 1-56065-304-3
    1. Fighter planes--Juvenile literature. 2. Fighter plane combat--Juvenile literature. [1. Fighter planes. 2. Airplanes, Military.] I. Title. II. Series: Wings (Minneapolis, Minn.)
UG1242.F5S26 1996
358.4'3--dc20   95-11254
                                                    CIP
                                                    AC

Table of Contents

Chapter 1

Fly Fast, Turn Tight, Shoot Straight!

Y ou're on a runway at a secret Air Force base in Nevada, strapped into a new kind of jet aircraft. As soon as the control tower clears you for takeoff, you're going to take the ride of your life.

Seconds after leaving the ground, you're flying at almost twice the speed of sound. The plane veers through incredibly tight mid-air turns. You're pulled back into your seat and from side to side in the cockpit.

A F/A-18 Hornet fighter streaks into the sky.

Your plane is the Lockheed F-22. The F-22 is a high-performance jet **fighter**, one of the fastest and deadliest warplanes in the sky. The aircraft has a needle-shaped nose, bat-shaped wings, and twin tails. Its twin engines deliver high performance in all kinds of combat situations.

Like all fighters, the F-22's job is to protect friendly forces and to seek out and destroy the enemy. During a mission, the F-22 may be called on to escort slower planes, such as bombers or tankers. It may shoot down incoming bombers, ward off attack craft, or chase missiles. Or it may tangle with enemy fighters in a **dogfight,** or air-to-air combat.

The F-22 is the latest in a long line of fighter planes. Fighters have been used in all the major conflicts of the 20th century. But strangely enough, the fighter didn't begin in combat. It began with friendly waves and smiles, far above the battlefield.

The F-22 Lightning II fighter is also known as an Advanced Tactical Fighter, or ATF.

Chapter 2

The First Fighters

Airplanes were first used in battle during World War I (1914-1918). At the start of the war, the planes did no shooting. Instead, their pilots watched the enemy's movements and then reported back to their bases.

Even if they were fighting for opposite sides, these pilots thought of themselves as brothers in the sky. They'd wave to each other in their wood-and-cloth "flying machines" (the word "airplane" hadn't been invented yet). The

Flying F-16s, the Thunderbirds–an expert group of Air Force flyers–put on a spectacular aerial show.

fragile craft barely held together even at their slow cruising speeds of 70 or 80 miles (112 to 129 kilometers) per hour.

One day, some of these pilots started pulling guns and firing at each other. No one knows why or how it started. Before long, both sides began fitting their planes with machine guns. War had come to the air.

The P-51 was one of World War II's most reliable and potent air weapons.

The Red Baron

By the end of World War I, pilots were fighting great air battles involving hundreds of planes. Many pilots won fame for their courage and skill. One was a German ace named Manfred von Richthofen, also known as the Red Baron. The baron flew a bright red Fokker. By the end of his career he had defeated 80 enemy pilots.

One day in 1918, the baron met his match in Roy Brown, a Royal Canadian Air Force captain. Flying a British Sopwith Camel, Brown dueled with the baron over the fields of France. The two planes climbed, dived, and turned as smoke tails twisted in the sky. Finally, Brown sent the baron to his death.

Fokker Triplane

The Red Baron's Fokker Dr.I was built by a German company that today produces jetliners. But modern Fokkers and the Baron's plane have only their name in common. The World War I Fokker had a bulb-shaped nose and three wings 23 feet (7 meters) across.

13

The reason for this design is easy to understand: If one wing is good, three are better. The triple wings of a **triplane** create more lift and support the plane better when it's climbing or turning.

Fokker built the Dr.I by stretching cloth over a wooden frame. The planes were lightweight but also burned easily in a crash. (World War I pilots always went down with their planes. They thought parachutes were for cowards.)

The Fokker's drum-shaped, air-cooled motor produced just 110 horsepower. Top speed was only 103 miles (165 kilometers) per hour. But this light flyer could climb to almost 20,000 feet (6,080 meters) into the sky.

The Dr.I was armed with twin machine guns that fired between the fast turning blades of the propeller. Timing was important in this system. If the gun fired too early or too late, the pilot shot himself down!

In battle, the Fokker triplanes faced two-winged **biplanes** (two-winged aircraft) such as the Sopwith Camel and the Spad, a French

These F-14 Tomcats are modern versions of the fighter plane, which dates to World War I.

machine. U.S. and Canadian pilots also flew in the war. But they only used planes built by other nations.

World War I pilots invented air combat as well as the tricks to win it. One method was to fly with the sun behind you—and in the eyes of your enemy. Captain Brown used this trick to blind the Baron and to find his own place in fighter history.

Chapter 3

The Warbirds

By World War II (1939-45), single-wing metal airplanes had replaced the wood-and-cloth biplanes and triplanes. The engines of the new fighters roared into the sky with over 1,000 horsepower. Top speeds had reached 300 to 400 miles (482 to 643 kilometers) per hour. Some of these fighters carried up to eight machine guns.

The Allies—the United States, Canada, England, France, and the Soviet Union—fought

The F-86A Sabre was the first U.S. Air Force fighter with swept wings. The huge air intake lay just under the nose

The Hawker Hurricane defended the British Isles during World War II.

Germany, Italy, and Japan. During the Battle of Britain, Germany sent thousands of planes against England. The English pilots had only a few dozen Spitfire and Hurricane fighters for air defense.

The British pilots fought nonstop, day after day, as the German planes swarmed over their country. Sir Winston Churchill, Britain's leader, later said of his fighter pilots, "Never have so many owed so much to so few."

The U.S. stayed out of the war until December 7, 1941. On that day, Japan attacked the U.S. Navy base at Pearl Harbor, Hawaii. The Japanese planes swarmed over the base, bombing ships and **strafing** planes and pilots on the ground. Few U.S. planes could get into the air. On that day, American airmen learned just how good the Japanese fighters were.

The most famous Japanese fighter was the Mitsubishi Type O, or Zero. This plane was 20 miles (32 kilometers) per hour faster than any U.S. plane of the time. The Zero's secret was its low weight. It didn't carry the heavy metal armor that protects pilots in most other fighters. The Japanese aces just took their chances.

The F4U Corsair first flew in 1940. It reached a top speed of 404 miles (650 kilometers) per hour.

The Messerschmitt Me-262–the first jet fighter–posed a deadly threat to Allied bombers.

U.S. aircraft makers quickly rose to the challenge. They built big, new fighters such as the P-38 Lightning, F4-U Corsair, and F6F Hellcat.

In the Skies of Europe

Germany's top fighters were the Messerschmitt 109 Gustav and the Focke Wulf 190. The "109" was one of the first fighters powered by a **liquid-cooled** engine. These engines, which were long and narrow, allowed designers to streamline the nose (front) of the airplane. This made the plane faster.

The 109 was a strong flyer, but it had problems on the ground. Its wheels were spaced too closely together, causing many Gustavs to flip over on landings. The Fw 190 had wider wheels but an awkward air-cooled engine. Designers streamlined the plane by placing a long nose cone at the center of the propeller.

Other great fighters saw action in World War II. But the best all-around **warbird** may have been the American P-51 Mustang.

P-51 Mustang

As the war dragged on in Europe, U.S. and British leaders planned to deliver a knockout punch to Germany. They began sending bombers 1,000 miles (1,609 kilometers) across enemy lines to blast German cities. But enemy fighters were cutting the planes to pieces. The Allies needed a long-range fighter to fly alongside and protect the bombers.

Such a plane, with the speed of a fighter and the range of a bomber, had never existed. But that didn't stop California's North American Aircraft (now Rockwell International) and its president, "Dutch" Kindleberger, from building one in just 120 days. The new fighter was nicknamed the Mustang, after the wild horse.

Just over 32 feet (9.75 meters) long, with a wingspan of 37 feet (11.3 meters), the P-51 looked like the British Spitfire. Many Mustangs did use a U.S. version of the Spitfire's liquid-cooled, 1,500 horsepower engine. The Mustang

P-51 Mustangs carried enough fuel to protect bombers all the way to Germany and back.

With an armament of six machine guns, this Mustang carries the name of Six-Shooter.

was a mixed breed, but it had a toughness all its own.

   With fuel tanks that held up to 489 gallons, a P-51 could stay with the bombers all the way to Germany and back. In a dogfight, the plane could reach speeds of 440 miles (708 kilometers) per hour. The P-51 had six machine guns, plus bombs and rockets. One German leader said "I knew the war was lost when I first saw Mustangs over Berlin!"

Chapter 4
The Jet Age

T oward the end of World War II, a new German fighter appeared in the skies. The plane was fast, and it had no propeller! Enemy scientists had secretly created the Me 262–the world's first jet fighter.

A jet engine takes in air at the front, mixes in fuel, burns it, then fires the hot exhaust backward. This forces the plane forward, at speeds no propeller plane can match. The Me 262 outraced the speedy Mustang by close to

The U.S. Navy's Blue Angels flying team includes this F/A-18 Hornet fighter.

100 miles (160 kilometers) per hour!
Nevertheless, the Allies finally defeated
Germany in May 1945.

Postwar Jets

After the war, several nations raced to build
their own jet fighters. The first British jet

**The Republic F-84F Thunderstreak was an early jet
fighter.**

fighter was the Meteor, which shot down hundreds of German flying bombs at the end of the war. U.S. jets included the Lockheed P-80 Shooting Star and the Republic P-84 Thunderjet. North American Aircraft, the maker of the Mustang, built the F-86 Sabre.

The Sabre's wings were swept towards the rear, as if the wind had blown them back. This design added to the plane's top speed, which was 675 miles (1,086 kilometers) per hour. Canada built its own model of the Sabre, the CF-86.

Soon the F-100 Supersabre replaced the Sabre. The F-100 was the first of a new line of

Swept wings allowed the Sabre to reach 675 miles (1,086 kilometers) per hour.

jets with top speeds above 1,000 miles (1,609 kilometers) per hour. At such supersonic speeds, the plane actually travels faster than the sound of its engines. Observers see it as a flash of silver in the sky, but only later do they hear its thunder.

Fast planes can be hard to turn, so the new fighters were not designed for dogfighting. Some models didn't even carry guns. Instead, their pilots attacked with missiles—sometimes when their target was miles away.

Germany and Japan had been beaten, but the world had a new conflict: the Cold War. The United States now opposed Russia and China. These powerful nations were building some of the best fighters in the sky.

MiG-15

In June 1950, war broke out in Korea. The United States and South Korea battled North Korea, a nation allied with China. American pilots joined the fight only to face the **MiG**-15, a fast new Soviet jet flown by Chinese pilots.

The MiG-15, the top Soviet fighter, was a tough match for the U.S. Sabre.

MiG stood for the names of the plane's designers, Mikoyan and Gurevich. The engine in the MiG was a copy of a British design. But the rest of the plane was totally new.

With 33-foot (10-meter) swept wings, the MiG-15 could fly 684 miles (1,100 kilometers) per hour and as high as 50,000 feet (15,240 meters). This was faster and higher than America's best fighter, the Sabre. The MiGs would attack the U.S. fighters from above, slam them with twin guns and a cannon, then rocket back to heights where the Americans couldn't reach them.

But the Chinese pilots were poorly trained and often fled during a dogfight. When the MiGs did stay in the fight, the Sabres shot down eight MiGs for each one of their own that was lost. If the MiG pilots had been better, the outcome could have been different.

In 1953, the Korean war ended in a draw. The Chinese and Soviets did win one thing: respect for their fighter planes.

The Soviets sold this MiG-23 to Libya, a desert nation allied with the Soviet Union.

Chapter 5

Today's Jets

In the 1960s, America became involved in another war, in Vietnam. U.S. pilots flew supersonic, missile-firing F-4 Phantoms and other advanced jets. But the enemy had the smaller MiGs, which could twist and turn and elude hostile aircraft.

Against such maneuvers, high speed and air-to-air missiles were of little use. This was old-fashioned dogfighting—and the Phantoms didn't even have guns! The military had to

Two F-16s fly in a tight formation.

The swing wings of a F-14 Tomcat allow the pilot to adjust the plane's shape for better flying.

attach gun pods to the Phantoms like spare tires.

U.S. leaders decided that the next wave of U.S. fighters would have supersonic speed, missiles, and the ability to dogfight. Grumman, a builder of Navy fighters, fitted their F-14 Tomcat (the jet Tom Cruise flew in the movie *Top Gun*) with **swing wings**. The pilot could

spread the wings for better lift at slow speeds,
or sweep them back for supersonic speed.

The Tomcat also carried a new **radar**
system. Radar can locate enemy planes in flight
and help the pilot shoot them down. An
antenna fires an electrical beam into the air.
When the beam hits a plane, it bounces back.
The radar system's computers read the

returning "echo" and show the target's location on a screen.

With its radar system, an F-14 can track 24 targets at once. The pilot can fire missiles at targets 100 miles away and still dogfight. With twin engines and twin tails, the pilot also has backup power and control if one side of the plane gets shot up. Other new aircraft, including America's F-15 Eagle, F/A-18 Hornet, and the Soviet Union's new MiG-29 and Su-27 fighters, also have twin tails.

If you see a MiG-29 fly at an air show, you'll probably see a maneuver called the

A crew of mechanics works on a twin-tailed Soviet Su-27.

The F-16 carries a heavy armament of missiles.

"cobra." Jetting along at high speed, the plane will suddenly slow down and almost stop in mid-air. As the plane hangs in space, the nose rises like a viper about to strike, then drops again before the jet continues on its way.

F-16 Flying Falcon

During the 1970s, aircraft designers began to realize how big, heavy, and expensive fighter planes had become. Some decided to try an idea from the days of the Fokker triplane. They would keep the plane light and simple.

One such plane is the F-16 Fighting Falcon. Instead of building the Falcon with swing wings, its makers turned the whole plane into a wing. The flat, wide body acts as part of the lifting surface.

F-16 pilots fly lying down, a position that allows them to withstand turning forces better. The cockpit windows let them see trouble coming from any direction. And the controls are **fly by wire**. The control stick is an electric switch that works computers that fly the plane. Computers make decisions far more quickly than a human pilot can. This is especially important when the plane is moving at twice the speed of sound.

The F-16 has only one engine. But because the plane is light, it's as fast as twin-engine fighters, and it turns tighter in a dogfight.

The U.S. Air Force Thunderbirds air-show team flies the F-16. When America's best pilots pick one plane over all others, something must be right about it!

The shape, color, and engines of the F-117 Stealth fighter make it almost impossible to see on radar.

Future Fighters

During the mid-1980s, ghostly shapes were crisscrossing the skies at night over Nevada. Some ranchers thought they were seeing UFOs. But nothing showed up on the radar at local airports. In fact, the ranchers were watching test flights of the Lockheed F-117 **Stealth** fighter. This plane is almost invisible to radar.

The 117's weird shape causes radar beams to scatter instead of bouncing back. Special materials also soak up part of the beam, so it never returns to the antenna. The radar sees nothing! When the U.S. fought Iraq in 1991, F-117s carried bombs right down the main streets of the enemy capital city. No one saw them coming.

But the F-117 was slow for a fighter, and its shape made it so hard to fly that pilots called it the "Wobbly Goblin." Many pilots were wishing for a dream plane with the speed of an F-16, yet invisible to radar like an F-117. That plane is the F-22 Lightning II.

F-22 Lightning II

Lockheed's F-22 is the fighter of the future. It has a top speed of 2,000 miles (3,218 kilometers) per hour—three times the speed of sound. It can also **supercruise**—travel at nearly 1,000 miles (1,609 kilometers) per hour for long periods of time. Its exhaust nozzles swing to the sides to kick the plane through turns faster. And though it looks nothing like the F-117, the new jet is just as invisible to radar.

Weapons are carried inside the plane, so nothing sticks out into the airstream to slow it down. The F-22's **fire-and-forget** missiles find their way to the target, even if the target changes position.

In the late 1980s, Lockheed rolled out this prototype of the F-22—the fighter of the future.

Computers track the plane's systems, so the pilot gets less tired. The information comes up on video screens instead of dials. Some key numbers are reflected on the windshield. This "heads up display" lets the pilot read data without taking his or her eyes from the skies. In the near future, the plane may even take voice orders from the pilot, such as "break (turn) left" or "fox one" (fire a missile).

The F-22 is the latest version of an old aircraft idea—the fighter.

A sleek F-18/A Hornet carries the markings of the Navy's Blue Angels flying team.

Glossary

biplane–a two-winged airplane

dogfight–a mid-air battle between fighter planes

fighter–a small, fast warplane designed to shoot down other planes

fire-and-forget–a missile system that allows the missile to track its target even after the plane that fired it has left the area

fly by wire–an aircraft control system in which the pilot controls movements by working a computer

liquid-cooled–an engine design that uses liquid to cool the heated parts

MiG–a Russian aircraft design company named for the two head designers, Artem Mikoyan and Mikhail Gurevich

radar–a system for locating planes in flight. Radar works by sending an electronic beam into the air. The beam can detect an object such as an airplane that crosses it.

stealth technology–systems that make a plane "invisible" to radar. Stealth technology includes aircraft shapes that scatter radar beams and materials that soak the beams up.

strafing–firing on ground targets from the air

supercruise–to fly at very high speeds for long periods of time

supersonic–a plane that flies faster than the speed of sound–about 750 miles (1,207 kilometers) per hour

swing wing–a movable wing that can be adjusted in flight for better performance

triplane–a three-winged airplane

warbird–a nickname for World War II military aircraft

To Learn More

Baker, Dr. David. *Future Fighters*. Vero Beach, Florida: Rourke Enterprises, Inc., 1989.

Cave, Ron and Joyce. *What About Fighters?* New York: Gloucester Press, 1993.

Richardson, Doug. *Red Star Rising*. London: Hamlyn Publishing Group. 1989.

Walker, Bryce. *Fighting Jets*. New York: Time-Life Books, 1983

Some Useful Addresses

National Air and Space Museum
6th Street and Independence Avenue
Washington, DC 20560

United States Air Force Museum
1100 Spaatz St.
Wright-Patterson Air Force Base, OH 45433

New England Air Museum
Bradley International Airport
Windsor Locks, CT 06096

National Aviation Museum
P.O. Box 9724
Ottawa, Ontario, Canada KIG 543

Index

Lightning, 20
Lockheed, 6

machine guns, 12, 14

Me-262, 25-26
Messerschmitt 109, 20-21
Meteor, 26-27
MiG-15, 29-31, 33
MiG-29, 36-37
missiles, 6, 29, 34, 36, 41

North American Aircraft,
   22, 27

P-38 Lightning, 20
P-51 Mustang, 21-23, 25
P-80 Shooting Star, 27
P-84 Thunderjet, 27

Pearl Harbor, 19

radar, 35, 39-40
Richthofen, Manfred von,
   13, 15

Sopwith Camel, 13-14
Soviet Union, 17, 29-31
Spad, 14
Spitfire, 18, 22-23
Su-27, 36
swing wings, 34-35

Thunderbirds, 38

Vietnam, 33

World War I, 9, 12-15
World War II, 17